OUT OF DARKNESS

POEMS BY
JAMMIE HUYNH

FREE VERSE PRESS
A FREE VERSE, LLC EXPERIENCE

Thank you to my mother and sisters whose light and love I would be lost without. Thank you to Colton for coming into our lives and helping us when we needed it most. Thank you to Dominique and Maria for always believing in me, especially when I didn't.

Thank you Jammie, it does get better and I am so happy you stuck around to find out.

ISBN: 978-1-7374696-4-3

Library of Congress Control Number: 2022936227

Author photo by Jammie Huynh
Book design by Marcus Amaker

Printed in the United States of America.

First printing edition 2022

Published by Free Verse Press
Free Verse, LLC
Charleston, South Carolina

freeversepress.com

TABLE
OF CONTENTS

MY MOTHER IS DYING

I lay in
the arms of grass,
cuddling close
to Mother Earth.
My cheek
pressed to
her soft, brown
specks rippling
with life. I am
flanked all around
by the dying
embers of abandoned
trees, gently carried
to rest by the soft
breeze. To my left,
the balding dandelion
waits to be freed,
while above
a bird calls,
but no one answers.

A GOOD MAN

People tell me my Daddy is a good man.
They don't know how he sheds that face
like a snake, hiding in the darkness
what he truly is. A devil

with crooked teeth and honey-dipped
words, chocolate eyes lure you in
to taste his bitterness.
He stumbles home drunk

swinging his Heineken bottle
until it slips from his fingers
into the kitchen wall.
He blankets the floor

with pieces of broken plates,
roaring, he paints our mother
in blacks and blues
that bloom like violets,

vibrant and colorful on skin
too soft and too supple.
He won't stop until he can
look around and see

the final masterpiece
of five children trembling
in the mouth of the hallway,
tears wetting the front of our

princess pajamas, frozen in place
by the horrific beauty of rubies
that dripped down the temple
of our mother like a crown.

Grateful and ashamed
that tonight, God has
chosen another
to suffer on his cross.

AMERICA DOESN'T LIKE HER PAIN RAW

with blood still dripping on the plate,
the image of Tamir Rice staring in her face.
She wants the meat without the moral lesson.
The poet puts on padded gloves
because America cannot swallow
bare-knuckles. Let me soften
my father's fist as it blackens
my mother's eye, so you don't
have to imagine that this is how
a child learns their colors.

America says she cares,
pinching the newborn cheeks of my oldest
sister as she gives her first cry,
she dazzles everyone with her voice.
But when my father's hands coerce
noises to rise from my mother's throat,
no one listens. So does that mean
she never made a sound?
If my mother dies
and no one gives a fuck,
was she ever really alive?
America will take us in
hungry and helpless
but only as compost.

America doesn't like her pain raw,
so she tucks it away in the pee-stained
walls of a three-bedroom coffin

where my father paints
my mother's cheeks rosy red
with a dash of violet,
an exclusive art exhibition
for their five daughters.
America gives him artistic
freedom but only if
he keeps us quiet.

America wants her pain served well-done,
dressed under different flavors
until the original taste is lost.
The blood is left out of the cake.
It is whisked into red velvet,
wringing my mother's body
for the food dye
sold for $7.99 a piece.
America profits.

America, I say,
My sister was raped,
but America rephrases:
She asked for it.
It sounds better.
America doesn't like
my father's name.
She changes Tai to Tony,
so he can clean women's feet,
because those three letters
are just not enough.
America gives my
mother a green card
but only because her skin
resembles a polar bear in a theme park.

My grandmother tells me,
Te amo. Pero
America stops those words
from reaching me,
ripping the tongue from
my grandmother to bury
with the other carcasses,
bleaching my speech until
the only words I speak
are the ones that leave me empty.

America doesn't like her pain raw.
She loves to watch us cook.

I DON'T SPEAK VIETNAMESE

When I go home for Tết,
I am greeted by the sounds of laughter
and karaoke in the driveway.
I can taste the spring rolls at the front door,
the smell of pho wafting close behind.
On the patio, my aunts and uncles sit
on the floor before plates of bánh xèo
and gỏi cuốn, their chopsticks twisting
in between blankets of white noodles,
their Vietnamese sharp against
my ears. I want to know what they
are smiling about.

In my cousin's house,
I am bombarded by lucky red envelopes.
Family friends I do not know
speak to me, but I cannot taste the
Vietnamese words they try to spoon
into my mouth, their flavors
lost on my tongue as my eyes water
from the heat of their accents
and all I know to say is

Tôi xin lỗi.

I am sorry.

I am sorry
that my father slept
next to cold bodies for warmth in hollow
boats that barely floated above
the water just to have his own daughter
be a foreigner in his family.

I am sorry
my uncles had to trade
degrees for nail salons,
changing their names
to American ones
like Eddie and Simon
just so their niece
could be an outsider
when they spoke in their shops.

I am sorry
my grandfather left his life
in Vietnam,
a photographer shot
in the chest by communists
for the pictures he brought to life.
He survived only to die
in America from lung cancer,
so his granddaughter could sit
on his bed and say nothing.

I am sorry
my mother's voice sings
in a different language and that
is the one I love best in.
Yo entiendo sus palabras pero
I want to understand yours too.
What is the Vietnamese word for "family?"

I am sorry.

My teacher colonized my mouth,
pouring Drano down my throat
to unclog my accent.
She set barbed wire against my teeth
and shredded the Vietnamese I wanted to say
until it came out English.

I want to say everything,
but all I know how to say is,
I am sorry,

Tôi xin lỗi,
and I don't speak Vietnamese.

MY MOTHER WANTS TO COMMIT SUICIDE

She is careful not to wake her husband,
rolling off the once white mattress that sits on the floor
beside the beer bottles and half-smoked Marlboro Reds.
She winces, unfolding her body
like the battered sail of a ship at sea
glancing down into the eye of the storm
at his pock-marked face.
The nosy streetlamps,
peep through broken blinds
as she wonders what it is like to sleep
without fear.

Her foot drags across the carpet
into the hall
decorated with dents
that would hug her perfectly.
She pushes open the door
across from hers,
knowing it is never closed completely,
knowing her children huddle
against its frame every night,
praying they will hear her voice.

Her children clump in the middle of the king-sized mattress
like gum stuck under the bottom of a desk,
awash in the glow of a green night light,
a mess of pink and blue blankets
surrounded by several long pillows
with the dark stains of tears and snot.

Her throat constricts at the sight
of her daughters,
sleeping like a pile of broken dolls,
five reasons she believes she's failed as a mother.

She limps into the bathroom at 3 AM,
the lights harsh, yellow hum
stinging her plum-colored face.
Her swollen fingers
reach for the pills
behind the mirror.

She throws off the caps,
stares into the red and blues.

Her body throbs,
one hand gripping the brown streaked porcelain,
her eyes too swollen for tears,

To die and to leave us
or to live with all of this, Mother,

  which decision scares you most?

WHY I STOPPED SPEAKING TO GOD

I remember the boy who raped my older sister
wore a gold cross around his neck. It would dangle
like a lonely noose reaching for someone to bow into.

I remember my father telling me about the floating coffin
he sailed in from Vietnam, a boy surrounded by
bodies and water, his hands a setting sun.

I remember my father's fist coloring my mother in
different hues of blue, and then I remember,
years later, in the aftermath of our Vietnam War

my little sister sprawled across our bed,
cuddling an empty pill bottle, my head filled with
how we would miss the bus.

When crouched under the covers of thick
red blankets in the midst of a southern summer
listening to the roar of my father's sermon
of obscenities into my mother's ears, I prayed.

I prayed listening to my sister gasp
for breath every night in her sleep,
never seeing the ghost that haunted her skin.

I prayed he wouldn't come home as my father
stumbled in every night, an angry
drunk that spoke with hands that flew
into my face, ripping the tears off my cheeks.

I prayed the Devil would take my father early,
the ground splitting beneath his feet, he would
feel the fear of his wife and five daughters
multiplied as the flames licked up his body.

God did not answer, but my mother did.
She stepped into the role of Jesus, my father's hands
the crown of thorns around her neck.

I stopped praying. My hands lay lonely
like forgotten land mines
one touch from exploding.

I stopped praying for a house
not crawling with roaches and mold.

I stopped praying for a father
that could leave dead bodies in their graves.

I stopped praying after watching
my mother's body stiffen, her limbs
retracting and face turning blue.

I stopped praying after I prayed to God
to deny her heaven
so she would stay to suffer
with us in my father's Hell.

Jesus was shoved into the trunk
of my car and God was thrown
into a fountain for good luck, to be
picked up by the boys with golden crosses.

God,
did you see how my mother's lips
bloomed roses at the corners?
Where father and her waltzed
dents into the yellowing walls?

God,

you were supposed to walk my sister home.
You were supposed to warn her
that the devil could be someone she knows.

God,

how come you only save
your sons?

MY 8TH BIRTHDAY

The candles flickered like
bodies swinging from trees.
My father hovered
just over my shoulder,
the executioner
in his pallid robe
waiting for the drop.
I sucked in as if I could
eat all the poison
out of our wounds,
and blew out—
trying to erase the crusted image
of my mother's bloodied lips
and the fairytale face
of my sisters around the table
as my eyes clenched shut.

I wish that my father was nicer.
I wish we were dragons and he stopped punching
her so hard
we could hear the crunch of her bone under his
knuckles.

I wish I was born a different animal.
I wish someone would save us.
I love my family, but the light
children were supposed to have blew out long ago
like the candles that could barely stand
against the breath of my 8-year-old mouth
and I want to wish it all back
because Cheyenne from class loves
going home to her mother without
bruises and I want to feel like her
when I get off
the bus.

MANDARIN

The bright skin of the mandarin
against the dark wood of the table
reminds me of an ember
drifting lazily from its home
to land amidst the grass,
during our summer night bonfires.
A dreary day of a monotonous routine
is somehow saved by the citrus fruit
whose skin is pierced,
by the blade of my nail.
I slowly peel away,
unraveling the mask it hides under
much like the one my father wore
when company came around.

The skin gives way to supple flesh
juicy and soft,
dripping onto the open wounds
of my knuckles
like the burn I felt
when my knees would skid across pavement
chasing my stupid cousins around,
under the gaze of a sleepy Helios.

One by one,
the pieces disappear,
like the afternoon days
of summer
when kids wave goodbye
to come in for dinner.

THE COPS COME TO OUR HOUSE AGAIN – STARRING BRUCE LEE

Bruce Lee is playing the role of a cop.
In this movie, he answers the 911 call
to a pale yellow house. He tries
to avoid the roosters and goliath-sized
potholes, passing cottonfields and railroad
tracks to get to the houses with
dirt yards and invisible people.

He pulls up to the house
having read his lines, already
familiar with what is taking place.
When he roundhouse kicks
the door open he is not surprised.

The scene is set,
shards of a mug surround
an overturned lamp,
the coffee table is flipped
over and broken plates
pile against the wall.
My father's fists are
still clenched into tiny meteors,
pummeling the center of our world
as my mother weaves in and out
like a boxer. The underdog,
we scream for her in
a corner behind the couch
the tears catching in our mouths.

Bruce Lee doesn't hesitate
and leaps, jumping across
a mangled computer screen
to one-inch punch my father into
the living room wall.
His body disappears and my mother
is still crouching, her arms a cross
above her head because she is unsure
if he is saving her or taking over.

Bruce Lee picks her up.
His muscular wings lifting
her off the ground immortalizing
himself in my mind.

Bruce Lee heroed
his way into my heart
as the father I'll always want,
the savior I wish could stay.
Stuffed under his arms,
he carries my sisters and I
to his cop car, placing us gently
in the backseat with his
powerful hands.
Learning for the first time
what a man could be like
even though for him,
this was only a role.

CUANDO MI MADRE HABLA

look at how she smiles.
A grin that took years to carve out of stone
is taken for granted by strangers
who try and pry her mouth open
so that it too, can be
properly colonized.

When my mother speaks
en su lengua, the timid lady
voice low and slow
disappears and the words
corren out of su boca
in a litany like
sus palabras are a wild fire
catching wind, raging
across el estado de California.

My mother thinks in two voices.
One in which she is una guerrera.
She slashes through the English language
her español to inglés diccionario in hand.
She was Theseus in the Labyrinth,
navigating through their, there and they're.
She slayed the minotaur with su accento,
the American dialect cut down
by the rolls of her Rs,
America lured her into the Labyrinth,
hoping she'd get lost in the myriad
of tenses and slang, she made beautiful
the ugly words they threw at her, growing
grass where they scorched the Earth.

And then the other, where
each word is a dammed lake
trickling off of her tongue.
People look at her
like she is dumb y *sucia*.
Ella sabe las palabras
that claw at her heart.
She knows what they mean
as they dig at the roots
she once proudly claimed.

Cuando mi Madre habla inglés,
it is like watching Prometheus
eaten alive after giving humans
las llamas de Olympus.
Forced to chew rocks in her mouth
when my mother speaks English,
be grateful that she is speaking English,
because she brings herself down
so los gringos may live more comfortably.

When mi Madre enrolls me in school
her hand clutches too tightly
around my 7-year-old wrist.
The teacher talks to us,
but I cannot figure out
which one of us is supposed
to be the child.
I stare at the teacher's yellow teeth
and listen to the tone that
drips from her lips. My
fingernails tear into my palm

and I squeeze my mother's hand.
The teacher's voice grates against
us, they don't know the melody
that follows the words my mother
speaks. They should listen to
the music that comes from su
boca when we are home
and how it sounds como un río
rushing through las montañas.

Mi Madre es una diosa,
brimming with a knowledge los
angloparlantes do not have
the key to unlock.
With no obstacles to trip over, las
palabras swim out of her heart
to dive into our ears, listen
to how she speaks when there
are no shackles on her speech.

She conquered the language
of Conquerors,
laying down flags in a land
that did not want her.
She planted herself,
digging deep into the earth
so that no matter how
many times they cut her down,
she would continue to grow;
wrapping su lengua
around their words
like she was presenting un regalo.
She rewrapped their language,
growing flowers in the spaces
between words and letters.

THE LANGUAGE OF FOOD

I can't speak Vietnamese,
my mouth colonized so properly
I can barely say my aunts' and uncles' names.
My mouth trembles at the thought of speaking
Vietnamese, it feels

like trying to kiss a girl for the first time.
My mouth sloppily presses against the words,
they tumble out of my mouth,
a tangle of syllables and tones.

I can't even say the names
of the foods I love, the ones
my aunts spill hours into making.
So instead of speaking, I eat.
I eat the stories my aunts and uncles
pour into their soup, their sorrow
seeping into the sopping
rice noodles, balancing their joy
in the swirling heat of the Sriracha
searching for its place in the harmony of flavors.

I wrap my tongue around the word Pho
slurping up noodles like they are a lifeline,
a bridge to Saigon, searching for a home
amidst the bean sprouts and cilantro
at the bottom of my bowl.

Their ships sail across the waves of broth
that bounce against the sides.
My chopsticks hugged by white noodles,
I see the bodies my family buried in the sea,
bean sprouts poking just above the surface.
They bring home a country thousands
of miles away from here, transforming
their memories into flavors.

Flavors that swirl in each of their children.
I love you is the full belly
of a child filled with thịt kho
and a steaming bed of white rice
with pork so tender it falls apart.
I love you is stirred into the beef stew
to take with you to college to ward
off the sting of winter nights.
I love you is placed atop the rice soup

when you're sick, decorated with pickled cabbage
and cilantro, the heat of it a soothing burn.
I love you is slipped in between the folds of the
bánh xèo they make, a Vietnamese savory crepe
with pork and shrimp. Their love
lays gently in the spring roll,
carefully wrapped in rice paper
but still filled to the brim.

They love with food and if I keep eating,
I can sometimes make out the soft voices of boys and
girls thousands of miles away.

TO OUR FATHER WHO IS BURNING

Father,
Did you mean to leave
your daughters ruined?
A gutted cathedral

purposefully abandoned,
beautiful but empty. We are
the ashes left between
the shattered stained glass.

We used to be a blazing sunset
but you left us a starless night,

buried in your shadow,
we are the victims
of your ageless anger.

Father,
Did we make you feel powerful?
Your fist connecting
with the bones of my
mother's blueberry cheeks.

Tell us
each bruise you branded
on our mother was
because you felt weak.

A sun-seared coal,
you burn everyone
you touch.

Admit it and maybe
we could forgive
you, or is that spine
of yours just for show?

Father,
can you see ghosts?

If so,
can you see us?

I wonder,
are you scared?

Staggering into the kitchen
in the hellish light of street lamps
that seeps through broken blinds,
you are a calamity

made of Heineken and Marlboros,
a lonely, drunk bastard
that cannot be salvaged. You see
children who are no longer there.

But we used to be.

I bet it hurts, Father,
knowing how Regret
will be the son
you've always wanted.

BELIEFS FOR SALE

We sold ourselves to God
for chocolate and cereal,
my mother sacrificed
her five daughters
so food could be
found on the table.
Every Sunday,
we went off to school
as specks of dirt
within a sea of snow
to appease the devil
in our belly
that scared our ribs
so much, they hugged
tightly to the skins
of our stomachs,
begging God to help
us get rid of him.

You fed us words
from the Bible
while our fridge
remained empty.
We ate cereal
where roaches had crawled
over the pieces of
stale Lucky Charms.
We rolled the verses of Paul
in our mouths
while we craved
the red everything
that fed Eve.

WHAT I DO NOT SAY

A few days after six Asian women
are murdered in Atlanta,
a cashier in Publix asks, *Where are you from?*
Her eyes never looking up as she scans my oat milk

and Red Vines. She does not see
the dark bags that weigh down my eyes
or the clenched jaw that threatens to spill over
with a *none of your business* and a *fuck you.*
I want to tell her,

I sprouted amidst Magnolias and Dogwoods,
and grew up in honeysuckle bushes. I drowned
in pitchers of sweet tea, surviving
every sweltering summer
in the South eating boiled peanuts
out of bags that dripped with water.
I grew up on burnt Waffle House coffee
and $5 Cookout trays at 2 AM.
I was raised next to cornfields and cows
and my cousins were born here,
and my family has been here for years,
but we will always feel like strangers—
won't we?
Hartsville, SC will never be the answer
because how could I
possibly be from here
looking like this.

I can't even speak Vietnamese. At each word that slips
something shrivels in my father's eyes,
raisins in the sun, his dreams realized

at a cost. His tongue catches
in the barbed wire of English,
as he tells me he loves me.
The words shred his throat
while shame bubbles up in mine.

Should I say
my father is from Vietnam?
Should I reveal how
my aunts and uncles
watched bodies sink into the sea
so they could come to America?

My family sacrificed their names
for the American tongue.
Simon, Michelle,Tony—
they try to only speak English
in their shops,
their Vietnamese an
attack on American soil.
Their nail salons,
once American dreams,
are now just targets.
I realize the first time
I will ever see my
aunts' and uncles' real names
will be when they die,
on gravestones or in headlines.

I want to tell her that yesterday
an old, Asian woman
was punched in the face

for walking down the sidewalk.
My grandmother lives alone in California.
She survived the Vietnam War,
her home napalmed and ravaged,
must America make her feel
fear in her home again?
How do I beg her in a language I can't
speak that she can't walk alone?

I want to say I used
to dream of whiteness—
of parents with no accents
and college degrees,
of food people did not look
at with disgust.
I dreamed of melanin
dripping off my skin
and a family that I
didn't have to worry about
because my nightmares
came true the other day.

I am not from
anywhere
but here.

Instead I say,

Me?
My family is from Vietnam.

The cashier finally looks up,
her eyes scanning my
face and nods, because that
is the answer she expected.

KNOCKOFF

I am the rubble my father brought
over, a piece in his pocket
when he watched his country blaze.
He tried to plant what he lost
in each of us but the hand
he used crushed our petals
and the flowers he wanted
wilted and drooped.
We were not what he wished for,
American knockoffs of Vietnam,
the words we don't understand
are a punch to his ego,
a needle in his eye.
He tried to build a new home
using the bones of his five
daughters and one wife,
but you can't use materials
that are already broken.
Father, I'm sorry that your
home burned away,
but please stop trying
to build over ours.

I WISH I WAS A BOY

My dad wanted boys so bad,
he tried five times,
seven actually if you count
my two dead brothers who never
crawled out of the womb.
I guess my dad never got
over losing the only children
he ever wanted.
We, his daughters,
the consolation prizes.

Well Dad,

I wish I was a boy too.
With my short hair
and flat chest,
I could pass for one.
They have great metabolism,
never have to shave,
and let's not even mention
how condoms are always free
and they don't get periods.

Dad, I wish I was a boy.

Maybe smiles would have
replaced the plum circles on
my mother's face,
your hands too preoccupied
with holding me, your only son.
I can just imagine
your bricks crumbling

like the Berlin Wall,
the stone falling from your cheeks
with a smile you could not contain.

If I was a boy,
maybe you would have
brought me to the hospital yourself
when I lay wheezing on the couch
instead of making us wait for a cab.
You would have cared
that I had pneumonia
and almost died at 7 years old
because I was your only son,
but you could afford to
lose a girl.

If I was a boy,
maybe I could have brought home a girl
without worrying your hand would
make the sun rise on my cheeks.
I could stop playing Prometheus,
and letting the unsaid words eat me alive
so that you could stay warm by the fire.
I could finally spread the lungs
that were cramped and decaying
with every breath I took
because I died a little inside
every time I had to introduce her
as my "friend."

If I was a boy,
maybe the other teenage boys
in school would have stopped staring
when my sister's shorts rode a little too high,
because they knew, she had a brother
they wouldn't want to fuck with.
They would stay away from my sister
at the after-parties for prom,
never marking her body like Cain
with stains that would never go away
and maybe then her soul would not be
weighed down by the echoing screams
of our mother that played on repent,
I mean repeat,
in the house we grew up in,
while they ravaged my sister's land
like the Aztecs who thought they had found God
but had been tricked by the devil.
Maybe she would stop trying to find
the broken pieces they stole
in the eyes of different men
that occupy her bed each night.

If I was a boy,
then I wouldn't have to see my sister's rapist
laughing in the halls at school,
because I would have been able to protect her,
and why weren't you the boy that protected her,
Dad?

If I was a boy,
maybe I wouldn't have the same cuts
on my wrists as my sisters,
like matching infinity symbols
from a pain we didn't know how to express

as you forced our tears down our throats
because boys don't cry
and you so desperately
wanted us to be boys,
and if I was a boy,
maybe it would have
stopped my little sister
from swallowing 30 pills
of expired Ibuprofen,
trying to fill the gaps
you burned into our bodies,
because if I had been a boy,
you would have left my sisters alone.

Father,
if I were the son you've always wanted,
I would've murdered you.

I CAN'T STOP WRITING ABOUT MY FATHER

I am trying to write a poem
that is not about my father,
where he is not even a cloud
or a ghost
or even a name.
But somehow, he bludgeons
his way into the title page,
knifing apart the letters
to make space for himself,
leaving so many inked carcasses
in the graveyard of drafts
beneath my desk.
He rips the pen from my hand,
intruding on the memories
of my mother's smile
as he frowns her face,
forcing her lips down
so all I can remember
is how he planted plums on her skin,
how each kiss,
seared into her eyes
and how his touch
sent worms writhing around her stomach.
Did my mother (because of my father)
regret my sisters and I were ever born?
I don't want to write that.

I don't want to write about my father.
I don't want his fists

bruising my memories
of playing outside with my sisters.
The five of us
wiping mulberry juices
on our shirts,
blue-teethed and
drunk off of honeysuckles,
we'd spend hours picking.
Cross-legged in the grass,
we sit in a rare silence
until my father's voice trumpets
across the backyard
and blows our laughter to the wind,
as dandelion seeds drift
to somewhere with better soil.
We force ourselves back into the wreckage,
sewing the pieces of our mother together
and wondering when we will be next.

I want to beg my mother
and sisters to stay,
and promise them
a different story,
a place in my poems,
a slice of the sun on a platter,
but my father has snatched
my poem away again
and like all the others,
dangles it above his lighter

until all of us are
just ashes
in the night.